FASHION FIGURES

KYLIE JENNER

CONTEMPORARY
COSMETICS MOGUL

Jessica Rusick

Checkerboard
Library

An Imprint of Abdo Publishing
abdobooks.com

abdobooks.com

Published by Abdo Publishing, a division of ABDO, PO Box 398166, Minneapolis, Minnesota 55439.
Copyright © 2020 by Abdo Consulting Group, Inc. International copyrights reserved in all countries.
No part of this book may be reproduced in any form without written permission from the publisher.
Checkerboard Library™ is a trademark and logo of Abdo Publishing.

Printed in the United States of America, North Mankato, Minnesota
052019
092019

 THIS BOOK CONTAINS RECYCLED MATERIALS

Design: Aruna Rangarajan, Mighty Media, Inc.
Production: Mighty Media, Inc.
Editor: Rachael L. Thomas
Design Elements: Shutterstock Images
Cover Photograph: Shutterstock Images
Interior Photographs: AP Images, pp. 5, 11, 13, 17, 23, 25, 27;
Getty Images, p. 7; Shutterstock Images, pp. 8-9, 15, 21, 28 (left, right), 29 (left, right); Wikimedia
Commons, p. 19

Library of Congress Control Number: 2018966459

Publisher's Cataloging-in-Publication Data

Names: Rusick, Jessica, author.
Title: Kylie Jenner: contemporary cosmetics mogul / by Jessica Rusick
Other title: Contemporary cosmetics mogul
Description: Minneapolis, Minnesota : Abdo Publishing, 2020 | Series: Fashion figures | Includes online
    resources and index.
Identifiers: ISBN 9781532119521 (lib. bdg.) | ISBN 9781532173981 (ebook)
Subjects: LCSH: Jenner, Kylie--Juvenile literature. | Fashion designers--United States--Biography--Juvenile
    literature. | Television personalities--Biography--Juvenile literature. | Women entrepreneurs--
    Biography--Juvenile literature.
Classification: DDC 746.920922 [B]--dc23

CONTENTS

A MAKEUP EMPIRE

Kylie Jenner is a reality TV star turned fashion and beauty **entrepreneur**. She is a member of one of the most famous families in the world. But she has also become known for her bold, colorful makeup and clothing. As a teenager, Jenner was famous for making her lips look bigger with lipstick and lip liner. Her **signature** style inspired the creation of her first makeup product, Kylie Lip Kits.

Today, Jenner runs the successful makeup brand Kylie Cosmetics. She also has a fashion line with her sister called Kendall + Kylie. Jenner's brands have made hundreds of millions of dollars and earned her international fame.

Jenner has been on reality TV since she was young. For much of her life, Jenner's fans have been eager to imitate her style choices. Jenner uses her fame and huge social media following to connect with fans and promote her brands. She is one of the world's most successful celebrity fashion figures!

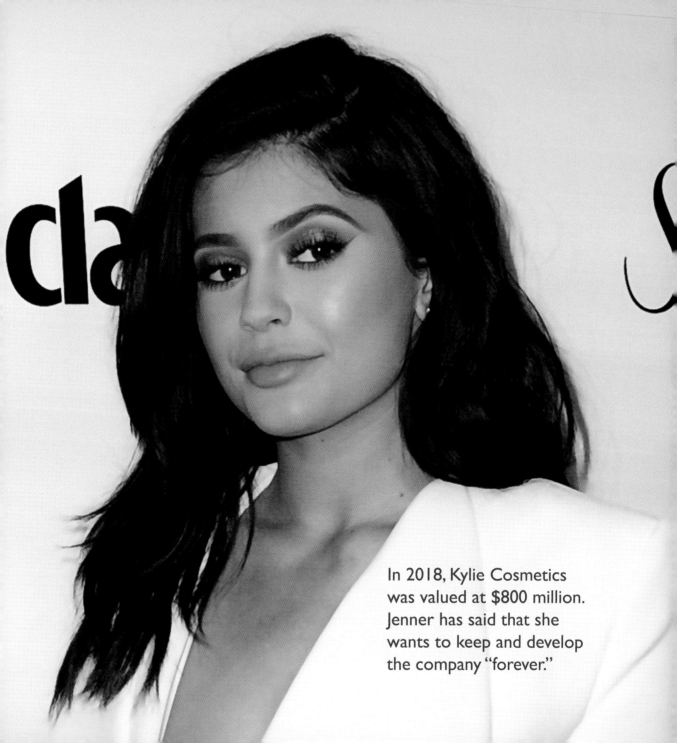

In 2018, Kylie Cosmetics was valued at $800 million. Jenner has said that she wants to keep and develop the company "forever."

FAME & FASHION

Kylie Kristen Jenner was born on August 10, 1997, in Los Angeles, California. Her mother is Kris Jenner, a reality TV star and business manager. Her father is Caitlyn Jenner, a former Olympic athlete. Caitlyn was known as Bruce before coming out as **transgender** in 2015.

Kylie has one older sister, Kendall, and eight half-siblings from her parents' previous marriages. She was raised in Calabasas, California, alongside Kendall and several of her half-siblings. These included Kim, Kourtney, Khloe, and Rob Kardashian.

FASHION FACT

Kylie studied from home with a private tutor for three years before graduating high school. This gave her more time and freedom to pursue her interests in fashion!

Kylie says it's hard to remember a time before she was famous.

From the age of nine, Kylie starred with her family on the reality TV show *Keeping Up with the Kardashians*. The show first aired in 2007. It follows the private lives of the Jenner and Kardashian family as they grow, interact, and build families of their own.

By 2010, *Keeping Up with the Kardashians* was the most popular show on its network. Fans of the show quickly became **obsessed** with every aspect of the Kardashians' and Jenners' lives. Kylie became famous before she was even a teenager.

Filming the show, Kylie lived and worked closely with her older siblings. So, she took inspiration from her brothers and sisters as they developed their careers. In 2011, Kourtney, Khloe, and Kim helped design a fashion line for the department store Sears. Kylie was fascinated by her sisters' work and encouraged to follow a similar path in fashion.

Kylie (*second from left*) with her sisters and mother (*third from left*)

KYLIE MEANS BUSINESS

Through her teenage years, Kylie became more and more famous thanks to *Keeping Up with the Kardashians.* At the same time, she followed her half-sisters' lead and became more involved in the world of fashion.

In February 2013, the Jenner sisters launched their first fashion line, Kendall and Kylie. The sisters helped design summery clothing pieces. These included **chiffon** tops, dresses, and graphic T-shirts.

Kylie enjoyed working with her sister on Kendall and Kylie. She especially loved researching fashion trends on social media. But Kylie also wanted to work on a solo project.

In 2014, Jenner turned 17. That same year, *Keeping Up with the Kardashians* reached its ninth season. More than 2.5 million people tuned in to watch the season's **debut** episode! All this attention and a little **controversy** would soon give Kylie an idea for her next business venture.

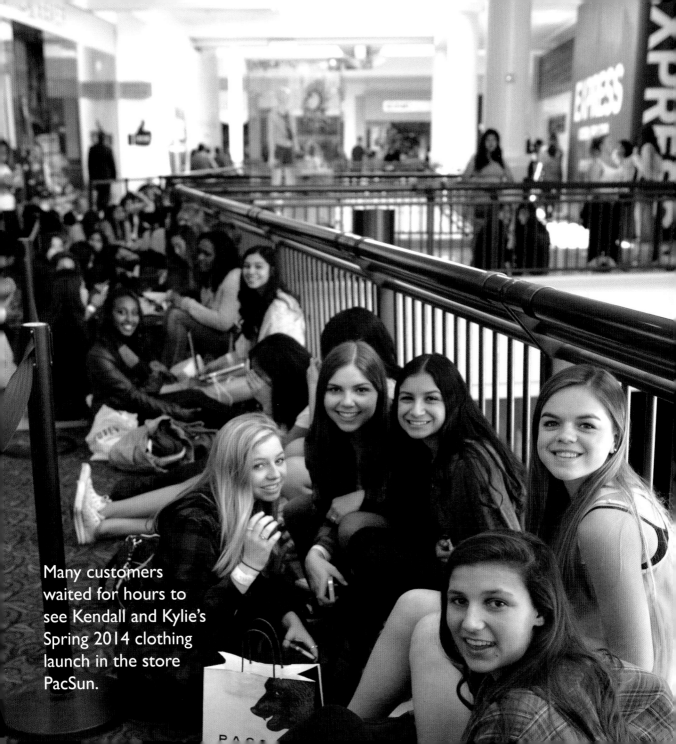

Many customers waited for hours to see Kendall and Kylie's Spring 2014 clothing launch in the store PacSun.

BIG LIPS & BIGGER PLANS

Eight years on reality TV had made Jenner famous for her **unique** personal style. Jenner was inspired by **vintage** clothing and liked to wear dark colors and leather. Wearing makeup to make her lips look big and bold had also become a **signature** look for her.

Jenner said the secret to her lip look was using lipstick and lots of matching lip liner. But as season nine began, many people noticed that Jenner's lips looked fuller than they ever had before. It seemed Jenner was using more than makeup to get her full lips.

Gossip magazines accused Jenner of using temporary lip fillers. These are chemical **injections**. The injections can add shape and volume to a person's lips for around six months. Jenner did not confirm whether or not she had used the fillers. So, the conversation around her lips continued.

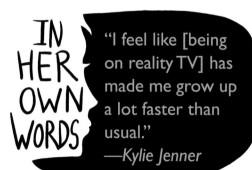

IN HER OWN WORDS

"I feel like [being on reality TV] has made me grow up a lot faster than usual."
—Kylie Jenner

Jenner says her makeup is "all about making yourself feel better."

Jenner saw a business opportunity. She could use the **controversy** to start her own makeup company! Kylie had enjoyed wearing makeup from a young age. It made her feel more confident. She began experimenting with lip products because she felt **insecure** about how her lips looked. But when Kylie searched for lip products, she struggled to find a color that suited her. She also found it difficult to find lipsticks and lip liners that matched.

Solving this problem would mark the beginning of Kylie's booming business in cosmetics. She had an idea for a lip kit that would let fans copy her style. Jenner's kit would include liquid lipstick and matching lip liner.

In late 2014, Jenner approached makeup company Seed Beauty to help bring her idea to life. Jenner paid Seed Beauty $250,000 of her own money to make 15,000 Kylie Lip Kits. It would take almost a year for the lip kits to reach customers. In the meantime, Jenner had another fashion project in the works!

IN HER OWN WORDS

"My brand is all about **empowering** young women and giving them confidence through makeup."
—*Jenner*

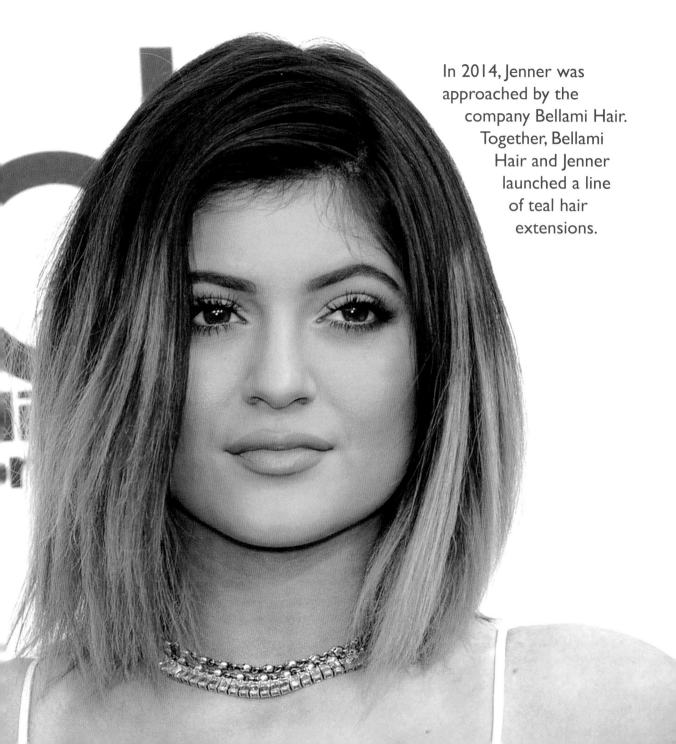

In 2014, Jenner was approached by the company Bellami Hair. Together, Bellami Hair and Jenner launched a line of teal hair extensions.

LIP KIT LOVE

In 2015, Jenner partnered once again with her sister Kendall. In July, the two launched a new clothing line, Kendall + Kylie. The Jenner sisters were gaining a reputation as young fashion icons! But before the launch of the clothing line, Kylie made an important announcement.

In May 2015, Jenner admitted to using temporary lip fillers. She said that her lip size was a personal **insecurity**. She was flattered that people imitated her, but she wanted them to know that it was okay to be themselves. She wanted to be a good role model.

Some people thought Jenner should have talked about her lip fillers sooner. Others wondered if she was a good role model to young fans. Despite the **controversy**, many fans were still excited when Jenner announced her Kylie Lip Kits were ready for purchase.

On November 29, 2015, Jenner announced the release date of her Kylie Lip Kits just one day before they went on sale. The news spread

KENDALL
KYLIE

The Jenner sisters at the launch of a new summer collection for their clothing line, Kendall + Kylie

quickly across social media. The next day, all 15,000 lip kits sold out online in less than one minute!

Many makeup users liked the deep, bold colors of Jenner's lipstick and lip liner. But not everyone was happy with Kylie Lip Kits. The kits got mixed reviews from some beauty **bloggers**, with some saying the makeup was overpriced.

But the complaints did not threaten Jenner's brand. Fans who were too late to buy Kylie Lip Kits in November desperately wanted to try the makeup. After the lip kits sold out, some people sold their $29 kits online for hundreds of dollars.

Jenner was quickly becoming a makeup **mogul**. And in the next six months, she would give her fans exactly what they wanted, which was more makeup.

FASHION FACT

Kylie Lip Kits were so popular that thieves stole them out of the mail! So, future kits were mailed in plain black packages. This made it harder for thieves to identify them.

One Kylie Lip Kit color is named Mary Jo K, after Jenner's maternal grandmother. The color is a bright red. This was Jenner's grandmother's signature lip look!

#INFLUENCER

In February 2016, just three months after the launch of Kylie Lip Kits, Jenner launched a full makeup brand called Kylie Cosmetics. The brand featured many new beauty products, including eyeshadow and eyeliner sets. But Kylie Lip Kits were still the stars of the brand. The launch of Kylie Cosmetics included 500,000 lip kits!

Though Seed Beauty helped make her products, Jenner was the full owner of Kylie Cosmetics. This meant she was in charge of nearly every decision. She came up with the concepts behind her new makeup collections. She also talked to the Seed Beauty team weekly to help design her products.

Jenner's makeup quickly became very popular. In its first year, Kylie Cosmetics made $307 million! One reason for this success was that Jenner connected with fans and advertised products on social media. This made her a social media **influencer**.

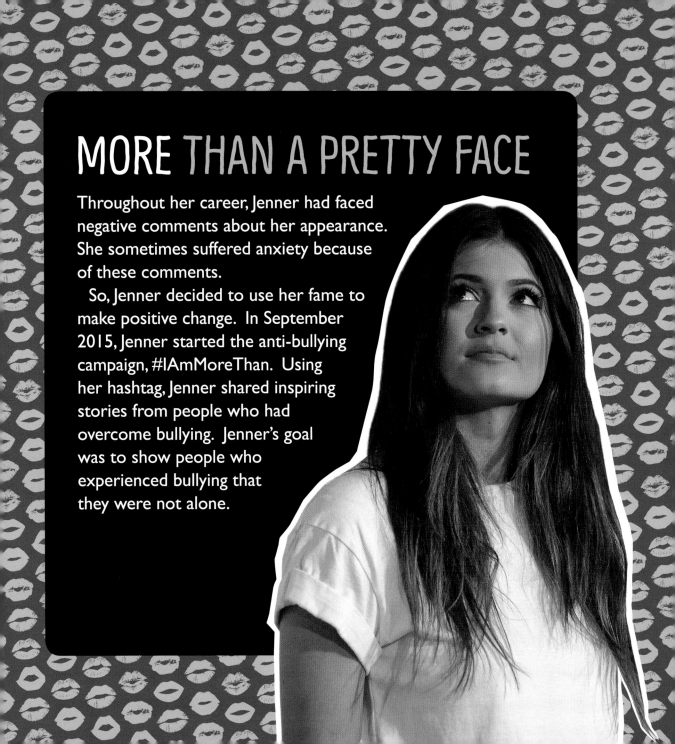

MORE THAN A PRETTY FACE

Throughout her career, Jenner had faced negative comments about her appearance. She sometimes suffered anxiety because of these comments.

So, Jenner decided to use her fame to make positive change. In September 2015, Jenner started the anti-bullying campaign, #IAmMoreThan. Using her hashtag, Jenner shared inspiring stories from people who had overcome bullying. Jenner's goal was to show people who experienced bullying that they were not alone.

Jenner's online popularity meant that she didn't have to spend money on regular advertising. Other companies often spend millions of dollars to advertise their products on websites or TV. But using social media, Jenner could share information about her fashion brands with millions of fans for free.

In between sharing life updates and style tips, Jenner used social media to tell her fans what was going on with Kylie Cosmetics. Fans trusted Jenner. This made them more likely to buy her products. Fans were also more likely to buy products that Jenner said she liked, even if she didn't make them. So, companies sometimes hired Jenner to say she liked a product on social media.

IN HER OWN WORDS

"Social media is an amazing platform. I have such easy access to my fans and my customers."
—Jenner

In 2018, the company D'Marie Analytics named Jenner the most valuable **influencer** on Instagram. The company estimated that a Jenner post praising a product was equal to a company spending $1 million on advertising!

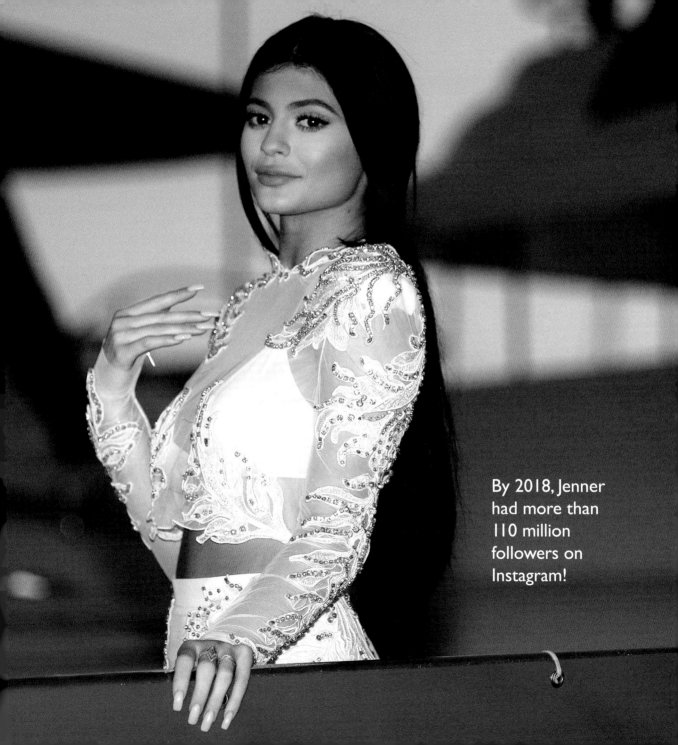

By 2018, Jenner had more than 110 million followers on Instagram!

KEEPING UP WITH KYLIE

Jenner and her brands continued to grow in popularity. To keep up with demand, Kylie Cosmetics released products at dizzying speeds. By 2018, Jenner's brand was selling 80 different products. Around once a month, Jenner also released new, themed makeup collections. She then promoted the collections on Instagram and Snapchat.

As Jenner's business grew, her family did too. In February 2018, Jenner had a daughter, Stormi, with her boyfriend, Travis Scott.

During her pregnancy, Jenner stopped posting on social media. She had wanted to keep her pregnancy private and special. Once Stormi was born, Jenner released a new makeup set. It was called "The Weather Collection," in honor of her daughter.

FASHION FACT

For one themed collection, Jenner's mom, Kris, "took over" the brand. On Instagram, Kylie Cosmetics temporarily changed its name to Kris Cosmetics!

After the birth of their daughter, Jenner and Scott released a YouTube video called "To Our Girl" that showed Jenner's journey to motherhood.

A RISING STAR

In August 2018, Kylie Cosmetics was valued at over $800 million. That month, Jenner was featured on the cover of financial magazine *Forbes*. The *Forbes* article reported that Jenner was on track to become the youngest self-made billionaire in history!

Jenner did not stop pushing her brand further. In August 2018, she said her goal for the future was to open Kylie Cosmetics stores around the world. Later that month, Jenner announced that Kylie Cosmetics would soon be available in Ulta Beauty stores, bringing her one step closer to her goal.

Jenner believes that makeup can help **empower** young women to feel good about who they are and how they look. She took this principle and turned it into a billion-dollar business that caters to customers across the US and beyond.

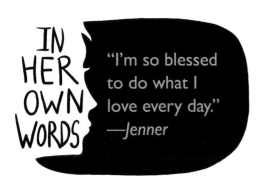

IN HER OWN WORDS

"I'm so blessed to do what I love every day."
—Jenner

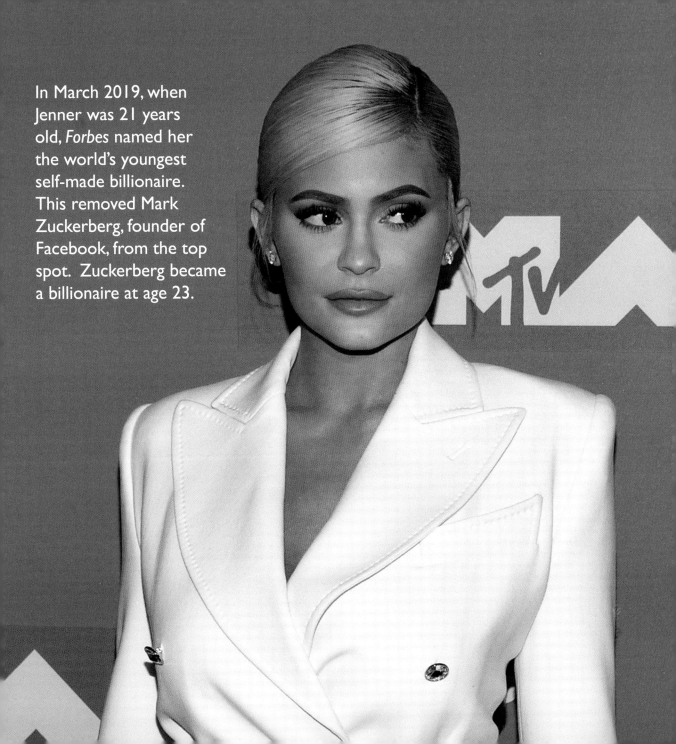

In March 2019, when Jenner was 21 years old, *Forbes* named her the world's youngest self-made billionaire. This removed Mark Zuckerberg, founder of Facebook, from the top spot. Zuckerberg became a billionaire at age 23.

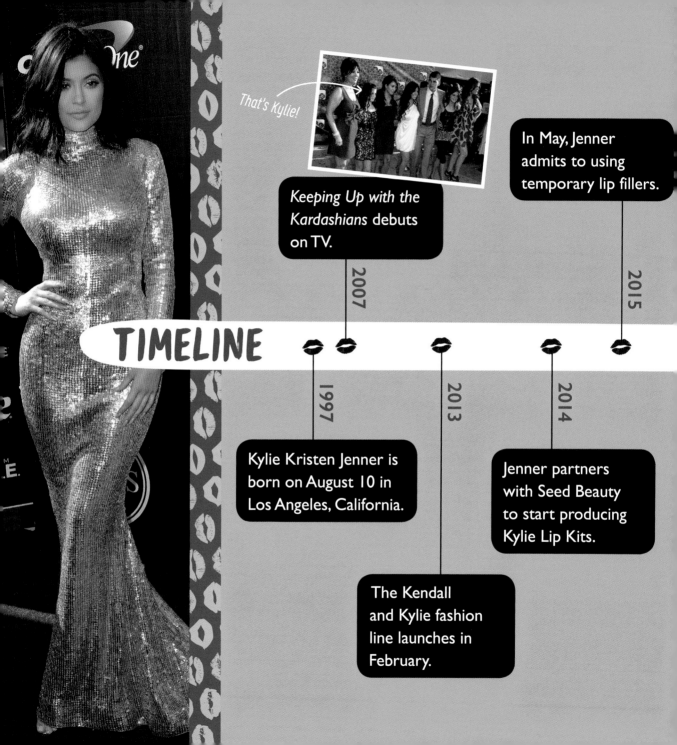

That's Kylie!

Keeping Up with the Kardashians debuts on TV.

In May, Jenner admits to using temporary lip fillers.

TIMELINE

2007

2015

1997

2013

2014

Kylie Kristen Jenner is born on August 10 in Los Angeles, California.

Jenner partners with Seed Beauty to start producing Kylie Lip Kits.

The Kendall and Kylie fashion line launches in February.

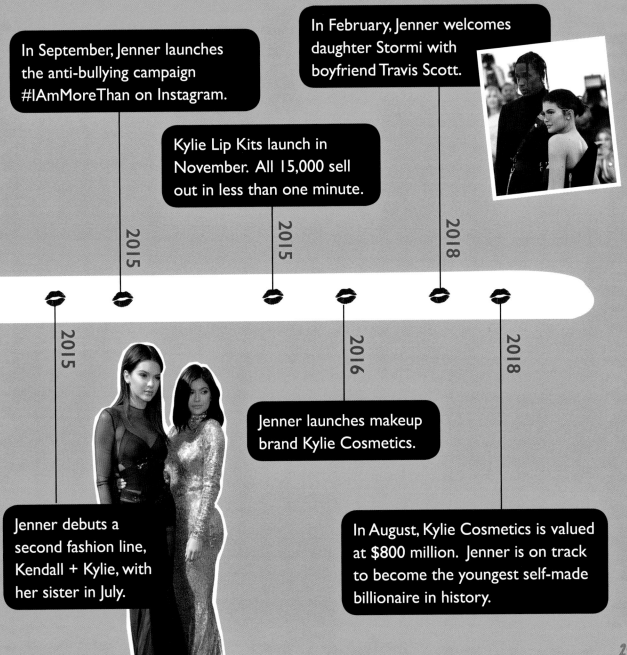

In September, Jenner launches the anti-bullying campaign #IAmMoreThan on Instagram.

Kylie Lip Kits launch in November. All 15,000 sell out in less than one minute.

In February, Jenner welcomes daughter Stormi with boyfriend Travis Scott.

2015

2015

2018

2015

2016

2018

Jenner launches makeup brand Kylie Cosmetics.

Jenner debuts a second fashion line, Kendall + Kylie, with her sister in July.

In August, Kylie Cosmetics is valued at $800 million. Jenner is on track to become the youngest self-made billionaire in history.

GLOSSARY

blog—an online story that tells about someone's personal opinions, activities, and experiences. A person who writes a blog is a blogger.

chiffon—a flowing, sheer fabric, often made of silk.

controversy—a discussion marked by strongly different views.

debut—a first appearance. To debut something is to present or perform it for the first time.

empower—to promote or influence someone becoming stronger and more confident, especially in taking control of their life and claiming their rights.

entrepreneur—one who organizes, manages, and accepts the risks of a business or an enterprise.

influencer—someone with tens of thousands or even millions of followers on social media.

injection—the forcing of fluid into the body, usually with a needle or something sharp.

insecure—lacking confidence or certainty about something.

mogul—a person with power, influence, or expertise in a particular area of business.

obsessed—able to think of nothing else.

signature—something that sets apart or identifies an individual, group, or company.

transgender—having a gender identity that differs from the one associated with one's sex at birth.

unique (yoo-NEEK)—being the only one of its kind.

vintage—old but still interesting or of good quality.

ONLINE RESOURCES

Booklinks
NONFICTION NETWORK
FREE! ONLINE NONFICTION RESOURCES

To learn more about Kylie Jenner, please visit **abdobooklinks.com** or scan this QR code. These links are routinely monitored and updated to provide the most current information available.

INDEX